SYDNEY
THE CITY AT A GLANCE

Mrs Macquarie's Point

Gaze out over the harbour from one of the best seats in the city: a chair carved into the sandstone peninsula.
Mrs Macquarie's Road

Art Gallery of New South Wales

Come here to see the largest permanent display of Aboriginal and Torres Strait Islander art in the country.
See p036

Sydney Tower

Venture to the top of this tower, nicknamed 'Centrepoint' by locals, and on a clear day you'll glimpse the Blue Mountains to the west and Botany Bay to the south.
100 Market Street

Sydney Opera House

The sails of Jørn Utzon's masterwork were said to have been inspired by his study of orange segments. He left the project in 1966, returning to it in 1999, to design an extension.
See p010

Kirribilli House

The official Sydney residence of the prime minister was controversially chosen by John Howard as his main abode.
Kirribilli Avenue

Museum of Contemporary Art

View shows, such as the annual 'Primavera', showcasing works by young artists, in this art deco building perched on the waterfront.
140 George Street

Sydney Harbour Bridge

Sydneysiders simply call it 'the bridge'. And yes, you can climb to the top.
See p014

G000275285

INTRODUCTION
THE CHANGING FACE OF THE URBAN SCENE

'It is beautiful, of course it's beautiful – the harbour; but that isn't all of it, it's only half of it; Sydney's the other half, and it takes both of them together to ring the supremacy bell. God made the harbour, and that's all right, but Satan made Sydney.'

Mark Twain may have written these words in 1897, but more than a century later they couldn't be truer. Sydney is nothing if not a tart – gaudy, proud, gorgeous around the edges but a little sleazy when you scratch below the surface. The Olympic Games in 2000 may have been the biggest party the southern hemisphere has ever seen, but the Sydney balloon still hasn't burst. The city – four million people of 180 nationalities sprawled across an area the size of Greater London – has seen rapid development in the past decade, a lot of it reasonably pedestrian. It's no wonder that a Sydneysider's favourite topic of conversation is real estate – who's buying, who's selling and, most importantly, how much money is involved. For visitors, especially the city and surrounding harbour, the raff-ish Kings Cross and Darlinghurst, the bordering neighbourhoods of bohemian Surry Hills and the more urbane Paddington, as well as the increasingly popular Waterloo district.

It is a fascinating place, with the added attraction that you can spend all day, almost every day of the year, in the sunshine. Many come to visit and never leave, which speaks for itself, really.

ESSENTIAL INFO
FACTS, FIGURES AND USEFUL ADDRESSES

TOURIST OFFICE

Sydney Visitor Centre
Argyle/Playfair Street
T 9240 8788
www.sydneyvisitorcentre.com

TRANSPORT

Car hire
Avis, T 136 333
Hertz, T 133 039
CityRail
T 131 500
Taxis
Silver Service, T 133 100
Taxis can be hailed in the street

EMERGENCY SERVICES

Emergencies
T 000
Police (non-emergencies)
192 Day Street
T 9265 6499
Late-opening pharmacy
Blake's Pharmacy
20 Darlinghurst Road
T 9358 6712

CONSULATES

British Consulate
1 Macquarie Place
T 9247 7521
ukinaustralia.fco.gov.uk
US Consulate
19-29 Martin Place
T 9373 9200
sydney.usconsulate.gov

MONEY

American Express
341 George Street
T 1300 139 060
www.10.americanexpress.com

POSTAL SERVICES

Post Office
Martin Place
131 318
Shipping
UPS
T 131 877
www.ups.com

BOOKS

The Fatal Shore by Robert Hughes (Vintage)
Sydney Opera House: Jørn Utzon by Philip Drew (Phaidon Press)
Oscar and Lucinda by Peter Carey (Faber and Faber)
Rabbit-Proof Fence by Doris Pikington (Miramax Books)

WEBSITES

Art
www.artgallery.nsw.gov.au
www.mca.com.au
Design
www.object.com.au
www.visualarts.net.au
Newspapers
www.smh.com.au
www.theaustralian.com.au

COST OF LIVING

Taxi from airport to city centre
A$35
Cappuccino
A$3.50
Packet of cigarettes
A$12
Daily newspaper
A$1.40
Bottle of champagne
A$80

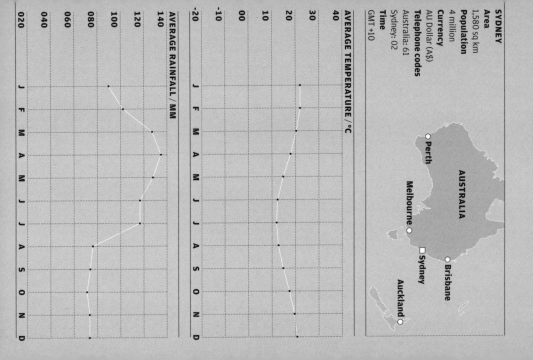

SYDNEY

Area
1,580 sq km

Population
4 million

Currency
AU Dollar (A$)

Telephone codes
Australia: 61
Sydney: 02

Time
GMT +10

AVERAGE TEMPERATURE / °C

AVERAGE RAINFALL / MM

AUSTRALIA

Perth

Melbourne

Sydney

Brisbane

Auckland

NEIGHBOURHOODS
THE AREAS YOU NEED TO KNOW AND WHY

To help you navigate the city, we've chosen the most interesting districts (see below and the map inside the back cover) and colour-coded our featured venues, according to their location; those venues that are outside these areas are not coloured.

BONDI

Sydney's world-famous beach isn't nearly as beautiful as some of those to be found to the north of the city, but it is *the* destination for visitors, as well as Sydneysiders, set on a fix of sand, surf and café or bar dwelling: call in at Icebergs Dining Room and Bar (see p050). It is worth noting that the folks who live in Bondi tend to gather exclusively at the north end of the beach.

SURRY HILLS AND DARLINGHURST

One of the most diverse of Sydney's centrally located neighbourhoods is the bohemian-meets-trendsetting duo of Surry Hills and Darlinghurst. This part of the city has everything – fantastic shopping, eating opportunities and people watching – and is home to the city's gay community. Much of the area is in the process of being revamped, including the dowdy part of Oxford Street that runs through here.

WATERLOO

This suburb, situated to the south of the city centre, is definitely on the rise. In recent years there has been an influx of residents to the many new apartment blocks being built as well as independent retailers who find the high rents of the more established areas suffocating. If you have a little time, walk around the neighbourhood and explore the art gallery complex, shops and cafés on Danks Street.

KINGS CROSS AND POTTS POINT

There's 24 hour a day action in Kings Cross, once the red-light district but, largely due to community campaigning, an area that has been partially cleaned up in recent years. Walk down Darlinghurst Road, which suddenly becomes Macleay Street, and you will find yourself in a much more genteel part of town, Potts Point, where the streets are lined with cafés, stores and glorious 1930s apartment blocks.

PADDINGTON

The east end of Oxford Street is not only one of the best places to browse upmarket boutiques, but, if you stroll along its back streets, it's a good place to see some excellent independent art galleries and examples of typical Victorian architecture. In the early 1900s, the terraced houses you'll find in the area were considered slum dwellings, but today they are the residences of choice for the city's cashed-up younger generation.

CENTRAL BUSINESS DISTRICT

The Central Business District (CBD) is not only home to most of Sydney's soaring office towers, but also its most beautiful parks, finest art galleries, restaurants and hotels. Head north and you'll come to Circular Quay on the edge of the harbour (you can catch the Manly Ferry from here), the Opera House, a revitalised bar and restaurant scene, and the historic area known as The Rocks.

LANDMARKS
THE SHAPE OF THE CITY SKYLINE

What do people see when they look at Sydney? Locals tend to become somewhat blind to the exquisite natural beauty that surrounds them, although when the sun hits the sails of the Sydney Opera House (see p010) at just the right angle or they spot a grouper (a friendly fish that thinks it's a dog) while snorkelling in Clovelly Bay, they remember how lucky they are. The main landmark, of course, is not even land but water: Sydney Harbour. Entering from the ocean between the North and South Heads, this massive area turns into a number of secret bays and beaches before becoming the Parramatta River.

On dry land, you can get a good overview of the city from the northern side of the harbour – the upper reaches of Taronga Zoo (Bradleys Head Road, T 9969 2777) is a great spot. Just to the east of the CBD is the Horizon (184 Forbes Street). No one is entirely sure what Harry Seidler was thinking when he designed this wavy residential skyscraper, which would look fine in the city skyline but sticks out like a sore thumb in its Darlinghurst position. In the centre of the city is Sydney Tower (100 Market Street), a 305m-tall communication tower that the locals call Centrepoint. If you have a head for heights, go from the street-level shopping centre to the top then take the Skywalk (T 9333 9222). On a clear day you can see the Blue Mountains.

For all addresses, see Resources.

Sydney Opera House

After 14 years of controversy, 'the Big House' opened its doors with a staging of *War and Peace* in 1973. Since then, it has become what some regard as the most important modern building in the world, even though Danish architect Jørn Utzon walked out in 1966 due to budgetary and creative disputes. However, in 1999, Utzon (who has never returned to Australia) agreed to help restore his masterpiece in an A$69m improvement plan. With his son, Jan, and Sydney architect Richard Johnson, he designed a 45m loggia to be added to the west-facing foyers. It was opened in March 2006. In September 2004, the Reception Hall was reopened as the Utzon Room, boasting the venue's first real Utzon-designed interior. *Bennelong Point, T 9250 7111, www.sydneyoperahouse.com*

Aurora Place

Italian architect Renzo Piano's first Australian project was completed in 2000, and the slender, curved form of Aurora Place stands out as a unique vision among the CBD's forest of uniform office towers. Linked by a glass-covered square that displays artist Kan Yasuda's *Touchstones* sculpture, the building consists of an 18-level residential block and a 41-level office tower, featuring fins and sails in an ethereal tribute to the Opera House (see p010). Elevated plazas that allow people to meet outdoors without leaving the building helped Aurora Place win two of New South Wales' top architecture prizes – the RAIA Wilkinson Award and the Sir John Sulman Award for public and commercial building – in 2004.
88 Phillip Street, T 8243 4400,
www.auroraplace.com.au

Bondi Beach

On a sunny day, as many as 40,000 people can swarm to Australia's most famous stretch of sand. It's not the city's most beautiful beach, but, as with seemingly everything in this town, it's all about location, location, location. Just 8km from the heart of the city, Bondi is a place for people from all over the world, as well as Sydneysiders. They swim, surf, sunbathe and stroll along the promenade

that runs the length of the beach. It even boasts its own television programme, *Bondi Rescue*, which premiered in February 2006 and follows the days of the Bondi lifeguards, the all-in-blue professionals who patrol the shore year-round. On the beach itself is another Australian icon, the Bondi Surf Bathers' Life Saving Club (T 9300 9279). Formed in 1907, it's the oldest in the world.

Sydney Harbour Bridge
It took almost 20 years for the design of one of Sydney's most iconic structures to be agreed upon, but the world's largest – but not longest – steel arch bridge was finally opened on 19 March 1932. It cost A$20m to build and was not fully paid off until 1988. By the way, all of its 134m (at its highest point) can be climbed through BridgeClimb (T 8274 7777) – just don't look down.

HOTELS
WHERE TO STAY AND WHICH ROOMS TO BOOK

There is no shortage of accommodation options in Sydney, but if you're planning a visit during a peak time of the year – say, during the riotous Gay & Lesbian Mardi Gras Festival (www.mardigras.org.au) in March – chances are you'll need to book well in advance if your tastes favour the boutique end of the market. The city centre is home to most of the big-name chains, such as the Four Seasons Hotel (199 George Street, T 9250 3100), and the InterContinental (117 Macquarie Street, T 9253 9000), situated in a beautiful heritage building, but the smaller, more fashionable hotels tend to be located in the Darlinghurst district. The Diamant (see p022), is one of our top choices, especially if your budget extends to the penthouse. For both dedicated business and pleasure travellers alike, Darlinghurst is the perfect base. From here you can walk to the city or the shopping strip of Oxford Street and are surrounded by some of the best bars and restaurants in town.

Bizarrely, for a city that prides itself on its beach culture, there are relatively few upmarket hotel rooms with an ocean view. Thankfully, there is Ravesi's (see p028), which overlooks Bondi Beach (see p013). It also boasts Drift, a bar with a huge deck perched above the beach, the perfect spot for a cold beer after a dip. If all the rooms are booked here, take heart in the fact that Bondi is a mere 15-minute taxi ride from Darlinghurst.
For full addresses, see Resources.

Establishment

While it might be located in the heart of the city's business district – which also means it's just a short walk to the Opera House (see p010). Circular Quay and the bars and restaurants of that area – there are enough entertainment and dining options in this hotel complex to keep most party animals happy. But then it is owned by the Hemmes family, who run a number of Sydney's better-known bars

and clubs. A visit to the hotel bar, and the restaurant run by the Peter Doyle, is definitely a treat. The hotel has 31 rooms, half with pale, calming interiors and the remainder, such as the Dark Room (overleaf), with a slicker, sexier vibe – black floorboards, splashes of colour and high ceilings. Go for the latter. *5 Bridge Lane, T 9240 3100, www.merivale.com/establishment/hotel*

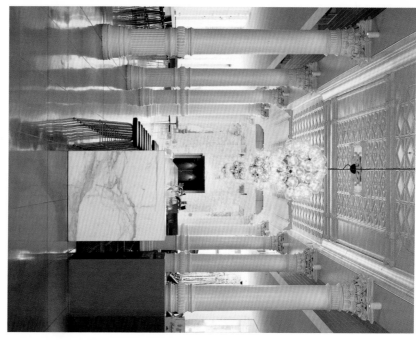

Dark Room , Establishment

Kirketon

Bought in 2003 by Eight Hotels, this is one of the city's most acclaimed boutique establishments. It's still extremely good value, especially considering its location and its recent update by Edge Interiors, which took the slightly masculine design and gave it a more luxe, moody vibe. Gone are the hard edges, replaced instead by modern chandeliers, leather sofas layered with brightly hued velvet cushions, and

heavy curtains. The standard rooms are perfect for single travellers, but couples with a penchant for spreading out should book one of the Premium or Executive Rooms (left). Rates include complimentary Fitness First gym passes.
229 Darlinghurst Road, T 9332 2011,
www.kirketon.com.au

Diamant

There's a pecking order of suites at the Diamant, which opened on one of the busiest intersections of Kings Cross in 2007. The latest addition to the rooms is the Penthouse (above and overleaf), opened in June 2009, an undeniably chic pied-à-terre designed by Burley Katon Halliday with two bedrooms, spacious open living area and two balconies overlooking the city and harbour – perfect for entertaining. While, the Courtyard Rooms and the Courtyard Suite also have decks with views down William Street, the other rooms don't have access to the great outdoors, but their smart, contemporary design by local company Edge Interiors is popular with business and leisure travellers. There is limited room service on the premises but there are plenty of dining options in the area.
14 Kings Cross Road, T 9295 8888,
www.diamant.com.au

Penthouse, Diamant

Blue

Taj Hotels acquired the W Sydney in February 2006 and rebranded it Blue. The 100 rooms, such as the Wharf Room (above) although a little small, are chic and luxurious, as one would expect, and the setting – within an old finger wharf at Woolloomooloo, originally built in 1910 during the wheat and wool boom – gives the hotel its unique charm. The Water Bar (left), with its layabout sofas and ottomans and low lighting, is the place to start and end a big evening. Great restaurants on the waterfront here include Manta (T 9322 3822) and the famous Otto (T 9368 7488). A favourite pastime is Russell Crowe spotting – the Hollywood star lives in the complex at the end of the Wharf.
6 Cowper Wharf Road, T 9331 9000, www.tajhotels.com/sydney

Ravesi's

Throw open the balcony doors and breathe in the sea air. All but two of the 16 sophisticated rooms at Ravesi's have views of the famous Bondi Beach (see p013). But even these two smaller rooms are comfortable (and budget-priced), thanks to the 2002 renovation by the designer Dane van Bree, who avoided the often-seen, twee pale aquas for this beachfront property and opted instead for a far more masculine approach. Each of the rooms is unique, with a black, copper and bronze palette and artwork. But the main attraction has to be the Executive Split Level Suite (above) – the only one with a full frontal view of that golden stretch of sand. Step out onto the sunny balcony and check out the vista.
Campbell Parade/Hall Street,
T 9365 4422, www.ravesis.com.au

Fraser Suites

This Manhattan-style all-suite luxury hotel was designed by UK architects Foster + Partners. Situated in the heart of the CBD (just minutes by foot from Chinatown and the city's retail heart), Fraser Suites has a maximum of only seven rooms on each of its 42 floors, which minimizes noise and movement from other residents. Each of the 201 rooms, from studios to two-bedroom apartments, has a minimalist design with luxe furnishings and original art as well as every amenity you could possibly need, including a kitchen (although there are no stoves in the studio suites). The gym features a full range of cardio and resistance equipment, as well as a 20 m lap pool. Breakfast is served in the mezzanine on Level 10.

488 Kent Street, T 8823 8888

Deluxe Suite, Fraser Suites

24 HOURS

SEE THE BEST OF THE CITY IN JUST ONE DAY

Ask 20 Sydneysiders how to spend the perfect day in their beloved city and you are sure to get 20 different responses: shopping, sunbathing on the beach, hanging out in a beer garden, checking out some of the world-class art galleries or eating until you are fit to burst. There is one thing you can be guaranteed – you won't be disappointed. If there's a cliché that sums up Sydney, it is this: there is definitely something for everyone. What you will need, if you're to sample all its delights, is an open mind, a lot of energy and a pair of shoes that isn't going to slow you down.

You'll want to make the most of the sunshine, the fantastic parks, the wonderful harbour, and some of the brilliant food and wine that the city is so famous for. So, get a good night's sleep (everyone needs one occasionally), then head for the beach early in the morning for a walk and to fuel up at The Shop (opposite) before going into the city. Here, we've incorporated a little culture at the Art Gallery of New South Wales (see p036), a sampling of Australian flora and fauna at the Royal Botanic Gardens (see p035), lunch by the water at Ocean Room (see p035), and cocktails at the Opera Bar (see p038). For those still charged with energy, it's time for a night out, Sydney style, in the clubs and bars of Kings Cross (see p039) – Gazebo Wine Garden, Kit & Kaboodle, Trademark, and Piano Room should keep you busy.

For full addresses, see Resources.

08.30 The Shop

The morning offerings along the beach at Bondi can be both overpriced and underwhelming, which is why you should make like a local and head to this hole-in-the-wall café on a side street. There are a couple of tables in the tiny room lined with retro wallpaper, but a stool under the awning on the footpath is just the place for a sunny start. Of course, there's great coffee, but it's the slightly offbeat

variations on some favourites – roasted 'shrooms' with feta and pesto, and BLTs with added gherkins and cheese – that keep people coming back. If you love the vibe, come back in the evening when it transforms into a wine bar.
78 Curlewis Street, T 9365 2600

10.00 Royal Botanic Gardens

Located in the Domain, the area south of the Sydney Opera House (see p010), is the Royal Botanic Gardens, Australia's oldest scientific institution, founded by Governor Macquarie in 1816. It's a beautiful place for a stroll and you can find, among many other treasures, an example of the Wollemi Pine, thought to be extinct until 1994, and tropical gardens growing in the two glasshouses, one a pyramid (above). If you follow Mrs Macquaries Road down from the Art Gallery of New South Wales (see p036) and towards the harbour, you'll find the information centre where you can get a map. From the gardens it's a short stroll to the foreshore. *Mrs Macquaries Road, T 9231 8111, www.rbgsyd.nsw.gov.au*

12.30 Ocean Room

A makeover by Japanese designer Yasumichi Morita, including a chandelier installation of 3000 wooden cylinders hanging from the ceiling, has given this waterfront venue at Circular Quay the extra wow factor. The menu by Raita Noda is equally contemporary and, at times, perhaps a little intimidating. The signature dish is called a tuna wing and, due to its complexity, comes complete with a map.

For the less adventurous, there's superb fresh sushi and sashimi, as well as interesting small plates for sharing. Try the curry pan, a deep-fried pocket of Japanese wagyu cheek curry. Unfortunately it doesn't serve lunch on the weekend, so instead take a seat on the deck at the MCA Café (140 George St, T 9250 8461). *Overseas Passenger Terminal, T 9252 9585, www.oceanroomsydney.com*

15.00 Art Gallery of New South Wales

Returning to the Domain, you'll find this impressive art gallery. It contains a large collection of Australian works, including pieces by contemporary Aboriginal artists, such as Ginger Riley and Destiny Deacon. The Asian exhibits are housed in an extension designed by Johnson Pilton Walker Architects.

Art Gallery Road, T 9225 1744, www.artgallery.nsw.gov.au

19.30 Opera Bar

By now, you're probably in the market for a cold drink. Watch for the crowd that gathers on the forecourt near the Sydney Opera House (see p010) and you'll have found the Opera Bar. It's an impressive destination with great views of the harbour and city skyline, and you really can't beat snagging a table in the enormous outdoor area when the sun is shining. There's also a much smaller indoor area with booths, low-slung stools and ottomans, and this is where you'll need to go to purchase your cocktail of choice. Every day, there's live music, from jazz to groovy beats. If you're feeling peckish, the kitchen does simple, seasonal fare, including charcuterie plates to share and great beer-battered fish and chips.

Lower Concourse Level, Sydney Opera House, T 9247 1666, www.operabar.com.au

22.30 Kings Cross

Until a few years ago there were few reasons to venture to the Cross, as Sydneysiders call this neighbourhood, unless you were after ladies of the night or illicit substances. A clean-up of night activity has seen a slew of clubs and bars open, dragging the crowds away from nearby Oxford Street. Early on, have a glass of wine and a snack at the eccentric Gazebo Wine Garden (T 9357 5333) and

plan your attack. For seriously cool cocktails, head to Kit & Kaboodle (above, T 9368 0300), two levels of fun inspired by Ol' Blue Eyes, 1920s Shanghai and Studio 54. There's also Trademark (T 9357 5522), underneath the iconic Coca-Cola sign, for all-night dancing, and its grown-up, glamorous sister Piano Room (T 9356 8238), where you can relax with waiter service and live tunes, from jazz to funk.

URBAN LIFE
CAFÉS, RESTAURANTS, BARS AND NIGHTCLUBS

Sydneysiders have a reputation for being somewhat, well, fickle. 'If you open, they will come' is the mantra. The problem is, they may only come for a couple of weeks before moving on to the next big thing. That's not to say that all new establishments disappear as quickly as they bloom, but what it does mean is that when a place is a stayer, it really is good. While the city has its share of big-budget interiors, changes in the licensing laws have helped a number of more intimate and individual venues open. For a low-key, but fun-filled night, we suggest checking out two Darlinghurst favourites: Café Lounge (277 Goulburn Street, T 9356 8888), which is almost like hanging out in someone's backyard, and Pocket Bar (13 Burton Street, T 9380 7002), a comfy, laidback spot behind an uninviting set of roller doors.

It is hard to say what nights are best when it comes to other bars and clubs. One Thursday somewhere will be pumping and the next week it'll be dead. The only general rule you can apply is that if the first bar you go to is quiet, it's going to be a slow night almost everywhere. A couple of things to remember: smoking is banned inside all restaurants (and in some bars and, increasingly, pubs) and BYO means 'bring your own' – wine, that is. In this section are some of our favourite spots to dine, drink and dance, old and new, covering the spectrum, from sophisticated to relaxed.

For full addresses, see Resources.

Rambutan

On entering this sexy space you immediately forget the Darlinghurst rabble outside. A long black communal table beneath Nelson Bubble Lamps draws the eye to the glowing onyx bar at its end. Up here, modern Thai fare – crispy duck with rambutan, eschallot, garlic and tamarind sauce; dry red curry of roasted pork belly with snake beans and holy basil – comes out of the excellent kitchen. But it is downstairs where you should go for a more relaxed vibe. People describe this funky bar – with aquarium at one end, Missoni flourishes and Florence Broadhurst wallpaper – as an upmarket tiki lounge. The innovative Asian-inspired cocktail menu begs to be worked through over a long evening. 96 Oxford Street, T 9360 7772, www.rambutan.com.au

Spice Temple

Descend into this city basement reminiscent of an opium den for Neil Perry's take on regional Chinese cuisine, drawing on the flavours of Sichuan, Hunan and Guangxi provinces. Red-hot chilli lovers will be in their element. There is also plenty on the menu for the milder palate.
10 Bligh Street. T 8078 1888.
www.rockpool.com.au

Mad Cow

Everything about this showcase restaurant in the Ivy complex has the potential to create happiness. There are the zingy yellow accents among a sea of white, the Astroturf carpet, the chipper waiters, the unsurpassed people-watching after dark as the bar outside fills to capacity, even the slightly kooky moniker. Then there are the grilled steaks – there's a choice of many, including Wagyu – done any way you please. Chef Chris Whitehead's skills aren't spent merely barbecuing beef though; there's also a range of seafood dishes and a vegetarian option. Like all the venues at Ivy, Mad Cow has its detractors, most of whom say it's just way too expensive, especially when steaks come served only with lemon and béarnaise. Bah humbug, we say. Enjoy the exuberant atmosphere and treat yourself.
330 George Street, T 9240 3000,
www.merivale.com

Bodega Tapas

Every night of the week (except Sunday) diners vie for one of the snug tables or a stool at the counter in this popular tapas bar that opened in 2006. Thankfully, in more recent years, owner-chefs Ben Milgate and Elvis Abrahanowicz have taken over the space next door to create a small bar for waiting patrons. While the menu leans heavily towards Spain — 'fish fingers' of sashimi kingfish on garlic toast with cuttlefish ceviche and dried tuna are two dishes that shouldn't be missed — there are South American influences too, in the form of empanadas and corn tamales with black beans and avocado. Wondering what the Spanish phrase on the bull mural says? 'Full belly, content heart.' We couldn't agree more.
216 Commonwealth Street, T 9212 7766, www.bodegatapas.com

Bentley Restaurant & Bar

Molecular gastronomy sounds somehow dated but one of the few survivors on the local scene is chef Brent Savage's Bentley. In this corner bar/restaurant, decorated with laser-cut plywood and dashes of red, you can pop in for a glass of wine from a stellar global list edited by sommelier Nick Hildebrandt (who co-owns the place with Savage) and a dish of warm olives, or make a night of it. Highly recommended is the eight-course tasting menu, a flavourful flight of fancy. Dishes could include black sesame and pea fondant with snow peas and goat's curd, and white chocolate mousse with pear sorbet and eucalyptus. It might sound like culinary élitism but the crowd is mixed and the atmosphere is always buzzing. *320 Crown Street, T 9332 2344, www.thebentley.com.au*

The Winery

The bar's owners have installed an Enomatic wine system, which allows them to offer more than 50 choices by the glass, and have barrels of 'guest' wine shipped down from the Hunter Valley each week. The wine list here is serious, but no one at this bar takes themselves too seriously. *285A Crown Street, T 9331 0833, www.thegazebos.com.au*

Icebergs Dining Room and Bar

When paparazzi shots of visiting movie stars and singers appear in the local newpapers, the celebs in question have invariably been caught outside this venue, which was designed by Italian architect Claudio Lazzarini and Australian architect Carl Pickering. Lots of attention has been paid to this prime piece of real estate, opened in 2002 and run by restaurateur Maurice Terzini, not least because of its enviable position perched high over the southern end of Bondi Beach (see p013). This is one of the coolest places in the city to sup, while the restaurant, which serves modern Mediterranean fare, with an emphasis on seafood, is first-class. You can hardly go wrong with the extensive wine list, either. Go on a week night when it's a little quieter, and hang out with the locals having cocktails in the chi-chi bar.
1 Notts Avenue, T 9365 9000,
www.idrb.com

Rum Diaries

No prizes for guessing that the brains behind this operation are obsessed with rum and, to that end, they've gathered something like 90 different varieties behind the bar. You can order any number of rum-based cocktails, including the ubiquitous but excellent mojito, a hot buttered rum for when the night is cold, and a zombie for when you're feeling a little deathly. The bar's three rooms have a moody, dark vibe with candle light, a piano in one corner and many attractive young locals perched on ottomans and chairs. The rum doesn't end on the cocktail menu either. The 'fusion tapas' include organic salmon ceviche dressed with Bloody Mary jelly cubes and an assiette of rum and chocolate.

288 Bondi Road, T 9300 0440,
www.therumdiaries.com.au

Etch

Chef Justin North is much admired by diners and critics in Sydney. His first restaurant, Bécasse, has thrived, due to his deftness of touch and commitment to sourcing the best produce. North has taken those principles and applied them to the more casual, but still impressive Etch, in the InterContinental Hotel, the idea being to give city workers somewhere they could eat well-prepared, sustainable

food without breaking the bank. Arched windows, patterned wallpaper and portraits of actresses from the 1920s set the scene but don't distract from the real star of the show: the European menu, overseen by chef James Metcalfe and borrowing from the regional cuisines of France, Italy and Spain.
62 Bridge Street, T 9247 4777, www.etchdining.com

Sticky

Finding this bar is half the fun. You need to go to the back of the building, down Taggarts Lane, and make a phone call at the door to get someone to let you in. Once you've climbed the stairs, find a squishy armchair and enjoy. There's a good selection of wine, some Italian beers and perfectly mixed cocktails; the house special is of course 'the sticky'.

182 Campbell Street, T 416 096 916

Toko

There are 20,000 matches in Reni Kung's sculpture-cum-light on the wall of the wood-lined bar at Toko. Seeing such craftsmanship is worth a visit alone, but take a seat here and indulge in one of the cocktails before heading into the dining room. You can sit either at a communal table or on a stool along the sushi bar to enjoy the *izakaya*-style dining. The room hums with conversation as waiters

deliver plates of supremely fresh sushi and sashimi to groups of fashionable youngsters. Like the finely manicured room, every plate that's presented is so elegant and pristine, it almost seems an insult to the kitchen to devour them, but we dare you to resist the crispy soft-shell crab served with a wasabi mayonnaise. *490 Crown Street, T 9357 6100, www.toko.com.au*

Ruby Rabbit
Across its three floors Ruby Rabbit offers a little bit of everything. There's the bar of that particular name in the middle, the rather posh and exclusive De Nom on the top floor, and on the ground floor is Big Rig Diner (pictured). The open kitchen serves classics like burgers, hot dogs and chilli fries.
231 Oxford Street. T 9326 0044.
www.rubyrabbit.com.au

North Bondi Italian Food

It's a case of share and share alike at the north end of Bondi, where – not satisfied with already having the best venue in the area (the Icebergs Dining Room and Bar, see p050) – Maurice Terzini and chef Robert Marchetti have taken over the space underneath the North Bondi RSL Club (T 9130 3152). Order plates of roast suckling meats, calamari, baccalà (salted cod) balls and Italian cheeses, then place them in the middle of the table, so everyone gets a taste. The vibe is casual in this trattoria-style venue, but it's still as cool as, well, Icebergs. Arrive early (or hold out for a late supper), as there is a no-reservations policy.
120 Ramsgate Avenue, T 9300 4400, www.idrb.com

INSIDER'S GUIDE
ANNA PLUNKETT, FASHION DESIGNER

Famous among Australia's fashion circle for being one half of the duo that turned down an internship with Galliano, Anna Plunkett is more than happy with her decision. She and Luke Sales, her partner in design, launched Romance Was Born in 2005 and their irreverent, finely tailored pieces are now much sought after. Living in Surry Hills keeps Plunkett close to Sydney's creative heart and some of her favourite places.

Plunket is a fan of Bourke Street Bakery (633 Bourke Street, T 9699 1011), where competition for one of the benches on the footpath is fierce – you can't beat it for a quick coffee and one of its famous pork and fennel sausages rolls. She describes the Cricketers Arms (106 Fitzroy Street, T 9331 3301), one of Sydney's coolest pubs, as her second living room. The crowd is eclectic, unpretentious and plentiful, particularly on Friday night. Visitors from out of town get taken to another pub, the Glenmore Hotel (96 Cumberland Street, T 9247 4794). Even though it's been in The Rocks since 1921, it's still something of a secret, even among locals. 'The rooftop has a really good vibe and great views over the harbour and Opera House,' Plunkett says. For a special occasion, she's a recent convert to Rockpool Bar & Grill (66 Hunter Street, T 8078 1900). Plunkett also likes Pasteur (790 George Street, T 9212 5622), which might not be glam, but the phò is the best in Sydney. *For full addresses, see Resources.*

ARCHITOUR
A GUIDE TO SYDNEY'S ICONIC BUILDINGS

Just over 200 years have elapsed since it was colonised, and Sydney does not have the diverse architectural offerings of many cities its size. What it does have, however, are some very interesting examples of art deco, modernist and contemporary buildings, designed by both Australian and overseas architects. In a city that prides itself on having one of the most beautiful harbours in the world, it should come as no surprise that much of the interest in development and redevelopment hangs around the water. For many, it causes concern and controversy – after all, it doesn't take a rocket scientist to realise that water views and private jetties equal megabucks for property developers, yet many community activists envisage important harbour sites being reclaimed for public use as parks, and recreational and cultural areas.

So, you have areas where important historical buildings, such as those located on wharves in the inner harbour that serve as reminders of the city's maritime past, are being rescued, while others are being visually vandalised. Take, for example, the apartment blocks built on East Circular Quay at the end of the 1990s – dubbed 'the Toaster' by locals – that block views to the Sydney Opera House (see p010). Here, we take a tour of the more notable examples of Sydney architecture – some highly visible and others a little harder to find, though no less interesting.

For full addresses, see Resources.

Sydney Theatre

In this theatre, opened in 2004, architect Andrew Andersons impressively marries modern design (in the asymmetrical foyer and in the slender balcony that overlooks the street) to the heritage elements of an old bond store, including restored walls of convict-hewn cliff faces (in the backstage area). For the audience, there are 850 seats covered in a purple stretch fabric rather than the standard velvet. Andrew

Andersons' firm, Peddle Thorp & Walker, also designed the Hickson Road Bistro (T 9250 1990) next door. A stunning red glass screen marks the transition between the two spaces.

22 Hickson Road, T 9250 1900,
www.sydneytheatre.org.au

Rose Seidler House

The house that Harry Seidler, one of Australia's most famous architects and an émigré from Vienna, built for his mother in 1950 is possibly the best-preserved example of modernist architecture in the country. The elevated, cubiform house is arranged in a U shape around an outdoor terrace and explores the relationship between indoor and outdoor spaces using glass walls fitted with timber frames that overlook the national park. All of the original appliances remain in the kitchen, and the other rooms are furnished with pieces by Eames, Saarinen and the like. Now part of the Historic Houses Trust, the house is open each Sunday from 10am to 5pm. It's 30km north of the city. Also check out the Seidler House (see p100).

71 Clissold Road, Wahroonga, T 9989 8020, www.hht.net.au/museums

Castlecrag and Middle Harbour houses

Contemporaries of Frank Lloyd Wright, Walter Burley Griffin and his wife Marion came to Australia from the USA in 1914, after winning a competition to design the nation's capital, Canberra. When things didn't go to plan – bureaucrats and the First World War among the obstacles – they decided to adapt their principles to a large parcel of land in the Castlecrag area. There are 16 Griffin buildings situated on Edinburgh Road: The Parapet and The Barbette (including the Castlecrag Private Hospital at number 150), which were all built between 1921 and 1924. In the same area are houses by Neville Gruzman (17 North Arm Road) and Hugh Buhrich (375 Edinburgh Road, right). Although not open to the public, many of these buildings are visible from the street. Graham Jahn's *Guide to Sydney Architecture* (Watermark Press) has a map that you can follow.

Ivy Building

Revealed one glorious stage at a time
from February 2008, the Ivy building,
Justin Hemmes' temple to hedonism,
has already won several Australian
architectural and design awards. The
20,000 sq m space integrates boutique
retail, bars, restaurants, a function
venue, penthouses, and a rooftop pool.
*330 George Street, T 9240 3000,
www.merivale.com*

SHOPPING

THE BEST RETAIL THERAPY AND WHAT TO BUY

From huge, faceless malls covering more acreage than any person could possibly manage in a day, to quirky neighbourhood streets lined with unique boutiques, Sydney can give your credit cards a complete workout. For those who want to shop all day, there is no denying the lure of Oxford Street, Paddington, where you can flick through tomes about art and design at Ariel Books (42 Oxford Street, T 9332 4581) or try on perfume and make-up at Mecca Cosmetica (126 Oxford Street, T 9361 4488).

The development around Oxford Street and Glenmore Road has almost become a showcase for some of Australia's hottest designers including Ksubi (see po78), Willow (3A Glenmore Road, T 9358 4477) and Kirrily Johnston (6 Glenmore Road, T 9380 7775). You will also find in the area the more recognisable Australian designers including Collette Dinnigan (33 William Street, T 9360 6691), Leona Edmiston (88 William Street, T 9331 7033) and Akira (12a Queen Street, T 9361 5221).

Of the more interesting department stores, search out David Jones. Its two largest locations are CBD (86-108 Castlereagh Street, T 9266 5544) and Bondi Junction (500 Oxford Street, T 9619 1111). And then there are the markets, the perfect place to fair-weather shop. The largest is the Paddington Bazaar (St John's Church, Oxford Street, T 9331 2646), held on Saturdays.

For all addresses, see Resources.

Planet

Ross Longmuir conceived his first Planet store in Melbourne, but relocated to Sydney in the late-90s, to a large Surry Hills showroom. Longmuir's own range of contemporary furniture is now displayed to its full effect alongside a large collection of local craft and design items. Among the highlights are one-off porcelain pieces by some of the country's best ceramicists – such as Robin Best and Liz Stops – as well

as textiles, blankets, art pieces and toys produced from local and found materials.
114 Commonwealth Street, T 9211 5959, www.planetfurniture.com.au

Koskela

Russel Koskela's Scandinavian heritage is at the heart of the furniture he designs which benefits from clean lines, quality finishes and eco-friendliness. Pieces in his Surry Hills showroom are displayed in homely settings, alongside art, homewares and accessories sourced from around Australia.
Level 1, 91 Campbell Street, T 9280 0999, www.koskela.com.au

Published Art

You definitely can't buy the latest Dan Brown or Stephenie Meyer tome from this Surry Hills store. In fact, you won't find anything on its shelves apart from the latest release art, architecture, film, fashion, photography and design books and magazines. Opened in 1999, it remains the bookstore Sydney's creative communities return to for inspiration time and again, since the stock, sourced from a huge range of international publishers, can change from day to day. Owner Sharon Tredinnick, usually found behind the counter, commands a wealth of knowledge and is always willing to order a title that she may not have in stock.

Shop 2, 23¼–33 Mary Street, T 9280 2893, www.publishedart.com.au

Via Alley

You have to admire retailers who, even when times are tough, work closely with designers and artists to create a genuinely individual shopping experience. Not only does it benefit them, but those of us carrying the credit card too. Ben Hsu and Jane Lo's incredibly cool Surry Hills store stocks fashion, collectible toys, rare cameras, homewares and hard-to-find 'zines and books. Cosmic Wonder, Note

to Self and Surface to Air are just some of the labels available, but also look for fashionable creations produced especially for the store by select artists and publications by VA Editions. Its first release is Short, an art-cum-colouring book featuring international artists such as Stefan Marx and Mike Giant.
Shop 3, 285a Crown Street, T 8354 0077, www.viaalley.com.au

Ksubi

Famous or infamous? Regardless of your views on Australian fashion's bad boys Dan Single and George Gorrow (seems their rats-on-the-catwalk show in 2001 will never be forgotten), their influence has spread far and wide. Denim – bleached, torn, splattered with acid and plenty of other variations – is the label's much-copied signature look, but in past years it has expanded its fashion empire to include eyewear, books, art and music. The Paddington store, called From Here to Infinity, displays it all, alongside some select international labels like Tsumori Chisato and Jeremy Scott. Single also DJs as Dangerous Dan, one of the Sydney collective Bang Gang – check local street press or the In The Mix website (www. inthemix.com.au) to see where their next party will be held.
16 Glenmore Road, T 9361 6291, www.ksubi.com

Paper Couture

There is beauty in stationery – intimacy, timelessness, delicacy – especially in the modern world where communication is most often immediate and electronic. This fact is not lost on retailers who specialise in handmade cards and letter-writing kits. The difference between the majority of these outlets and Jo Neville's Surry Hills store, however, is that Neville is also a paper artist who creates beautiful sculptures and more practical items, such as lampshades, from all sorts of leftover pieces of paper – from the brown variety used to cover school texts to foreign magazines. A coat made by Nelville from brown paper has appeared in so many magazine spreads it's now famous – so much so that he now makes a new 'fashion' piece for the store each season.

284 South Dowling Street, T 9357 6855

Hudson Meats

There is nothing more Australian than a barbecue, but to make it truly memorable you need to be putting the best of the paddock on that grill. Enter this upmarket Surry Hills butcher and delicatessen, located in a chic basement space. Owners Colin Holt, Jeff Winfield and Phill Mitchell have varying hospitality backgrounds but, most importantly, are aware of the consumer's growing desire to know the

provenance of their purchases. To that end, they spend time tracking down the best regional produce before adding it to their range. Here, you can pick up everything for a great outdoors feast: dry-aged Angus rump steak, Toulouse sausages, buffalo mozzarella, and a whole swag of swanky crackers and dips.
410 Crown Street, T 9332 4454,
www.hudsonmeats.com.au

Courtesy of the Artist

The couple behind this minimalist space, Nina and Cesar Cueva, have supported designers of contemporary jewellery and objects since 2004 through their Metalab gallery and studio at the other end of Surry Hills. This retail outlet is the perfect complement, selling jewellery and homewares, selected for both their beauty and function, by Australian and international companies and artisans.

Look for Mark Vaarwerk's necklaces made from recycled plastic bags, Cinnamon Lee's funky Black Boxes, Ben Edols' hand-blown glass goblets and F!NK Designs' matt anodised water jugs, initially created for a restaurant opening and now one of the most recognised shapes in Australian design. Cesar is a celebrated silversmith himself, so check out his designs as well.
547 Bourke Street, T 9380 9499

Assin

In a city well-known for its casual, colourful approach to fashion, the 2008 entry into the market by a Melbourne retailer renowned for stocking avant-garde international designers came as something of a surprise. But Assin's Paddington store soon became a must-visit for local fashion editors as well as international visitors (Kanye West blogged about it after his visit to

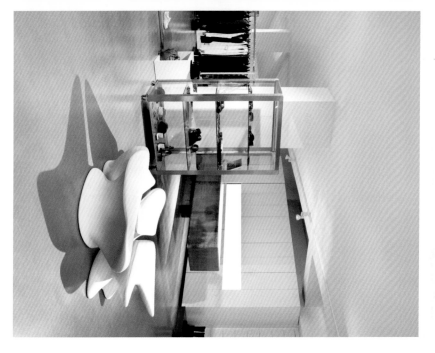

Australia). The visual style of the store can only be described as austere with its white walls and floors and low-key racking. Here, it's the fashion that speaks volumes, with labels including Anne Demeulemeester, Haider Ackermann and Rick Owens, alongside Comme des Garçons accessories and Beryll eyewear.
T2, Verona Street, T 9331 6265,
www.assin.com.au

Aesop

Designed by Rodney Eggleston of March Studio and company founder Dennis Paphitis, the contemporary lines of Aesop's all-white store are a breath of fresh air in the historic Strand Arcade. The full range of plant-based treatments is available here. Try the Rosehip Seed Lip Cream, perfect for the flight home. *Shop 20, 412-414 George Street, T 9235 2333, www.aesop.net.au*

Becker Minty

There's a little bit of everything in this lavish Potts Point store – fashion (Equita Negra for men and Day Birger et Mikkelsen for women, for example), art, ceramics, jewels, accessories, lighting, aromatherapy, stationery, even the most tasteful of bibelots. But it's not like you have to dig deep to discover something covetable here, because what owners Christopher Becker and Jason Minty have done is simply find the best of everything from across the globe. More recently the pair have opened Becker Minty Woman (T 8356 9908), exclusively stocking high-end fashion, on the corner of Macleay Street and Greenknowe Avenue.

Shop 7, Ikon Building, 81 Macleay Street, T 8356 9999, www.beckerminty.com

Saint Augustine Academy

Alvin Manalo is the head designer of this local label, inspired by indie rock and all of its offshoots, including punk, the mod movement and Goths. Collections are named after songs and albums close to Manalo's heart – spring/summer 09/10 was called 'Do You Believe Her?' after the Raveonettes number. The lines are sharp, skinny and sexy with monochromatic tones. You can find SAA threads stocked at some of the hippest boutiques around the world and on the backs of members of bands like Bloc Party, Wolfmother, The Bravery and Interpol.
642 Bourke Street. T 9690 2863. www.saintaugustineacademy.com.au

SPORTS AND SPAS
WORK OUT, CHILL OUT OR JUST WATCH

It's no secret that Australians love sport and the facilities in the city, boosted after the 2000 Olympic Games, are second to none. Water lovers are particularly spoilt with outdoor pools, often created around natural rock formations. Scattered throughout the city and along the coast, some of our favourites are the Andrew 'Boy' Charlton Pool (www.abcpool.org) in the Botanic Gardens, Wylie's Baths (www.wylies.com.au) at Coogee and the Bondi Icebergs (www.icebergs.com.au). Fitness fans seem to love boot camp, which has proved more than just a passing fad. Usually these involve a picturesque setting, a trainer yelling instructions and a group of keen people getting down and dirty at the crack of dawn. For information on local groups, ask at a nearby gym.

For those who prefer being a spectator, Sydney follows these basic rules: summer means cricket and winter brings football in its three codes – rugby league, rugby union and Australian Rules. Although thought of as a Melbourne sport, AFL got a huge boost in the city in 2005 when the local team, the Sydney Swans, brought home the premiership cup. Matches take place at the Sydney Cricket Ground (Moore Park Road, T 9360 6601). Also gaining momentum is the A-League football, with the home team imaginatively called Sydney FC (www.sydneyfc.com). Just a word of warning: most people still call it soccer in this part of the world.

For all addresses, see Resources.

Observatory Day Spa

If you thought caviar was for spooning on to blinis and that gold, diamonds and pearls were for creating elegant jewellery you've obviously never read through the offerings at the Observatory Hotel's day spa. Therapists exclusively use La Prairie products – if you want to look younger instantly book in for the 90-minute Pure Gold Radiance Facial. The Observatory Choc Therapy is exclusive to this location

and starts with a body exfoliation using walnut husks, followed by a chocolate fudge body mask and finishing with an application of chocolate body lotion. It's pure bliss. Leave room for a visit to the spa's excellent facilities, including a steam room, sauna and the 20m indoor pool (above) that sits below a domed ceiling. *89-113 Kent Street, T 8248 5250, www.observatoryhotel.com.au*

city Gym

This is the gym by which all others in the city are measured. It's huge, has been in operation for more than 25 years and has the largest free-weight station in Sydney. There is also an enviable timetable of classes, whether you're into yoga and Pilates or the action of aerobics, pump and fight-do.
107-113 Crown Street, T 9360 6247, www.citygym.com.au

King George V Recreation Centre

The site of this centre may be quite historic – it has been a sports venue since the 1920s – but Lippmann Associates' design for this recreation centre, opened in 1998, is nothing but contemporary with its curved steel structure. Inside, there is a fitness centre with classes from yoga to cardio-boxing, and courts for basketball, netball, volleyball and badminton, while outside there are basketball half-courts, tennis courts and a barbecue area. As well as being a sports centre for local residents and city workers, it is also something of a community social centre hosting regular barbecues and art classes.

Cumberland Street, T 9244 3600

Ian Thorpe Aquatic Centre
Designed by Harry Seidler & Associates, and completed in 2007, the centre is a collaboration between the City of Sydney and the YMCA to provide community-based fitness facilities. You'd never know you were at the Y though with state-of-the-art gym, three pools, sauna and steam room.
458 Harris Street, T 9518 7220,
www.itac.org.au

ESCAPES

WHERE TO GO IF YOU WANT TO LEAVE TOWN

You'll probably never find yourself bored while visiting Sydney, but if you're here for an extended period it's worth jumping in a car and exploring some more out-of-the-way destinations. Just west of the city are the Blue Mountains (the vapour emitted by the area's eucalypt trees give them that faint hue), boasting a string of villages – Katoomba is the largest, with Leura and Blackheath also popular stops for visitors – with antique shopping, fine dining and exceptional local produce. It's also the home of the Wolgan Valley resort (overleaf), on the far side of the Mountains, past Lithgow, in an area surrounded by national parks.

Naturally, the ocean plays a huge part in the holiday plans of Sydneysiders. Brisbane Water, a 90-minute drive north of the city, combines miles of great surf and pristine beaches and a series of stunning bays, separated from the open ocean by a craggy peninsula. Holiday homes line the waterfront at some of the quieter destinations, such as Hardys Bay, where life moves at a gentle pace. It's also where you'll find Pretty Beach House (see p102), a private retreat, with international service standards in an environment that seems a million miles from anywhere. Its biggest selling point, however, is chef Stefano Manfredi, who has designed menus that utilise the best produce from the local food bowl and who can often be found in the kitchen, particularly on weekends. *For all addresses, see Resources.*

Huski

Should the sun and sea get too much, the Australian Alps are one option. The region's Mount Hotham Airport is just 85 minutes from Sydney. Twenty minutes from there, within the ski resort of Falls Creek, lies Huski. This impressive boutique apartment block, designed by Melbourne architects Elenberg Fraser, is as far from the traditional Alpine chalet as you can get. The design was inspired by the

random angles of snowflake segments. There are just 14 apartments – from studios (with a spa in the bathroom instead of a balcony jacuzzi) to duplex penthouses sleeping up to 10 people – all featuring 120-degree sweeping views. During the ski season (June to October), no cars are allowed in the village. *Sitzmark Street, Falls Creek, Victoria, T 1300 652 260, www.huski.com.au*

Wolgan Valley

The Blue Mountains World Heritage Area is the setting for this resort, opened in October 2009 by Emirates. The spectacular site, 1600 hectares of former farmland, is complemented by 40 luxurious one and two-bedroom suites – each with plunge pool – all constructed out of sandstone and timber.

2600 Wolgan Road, Wolgan Valley; www.emirateshotelsresorts.com

Seidler House

Designed by the late Harry Seidler (see p066), the house was completed in 1999, is close to the historic country towns of Bowral and Mittagong and can now be rented. The four-bedroom home has a sweeping wave-like roof and a glass living area with views of the river valley. Outside, a wall between cliffs creates a natural swimming pool.
www.contemporaryhotels.com.au

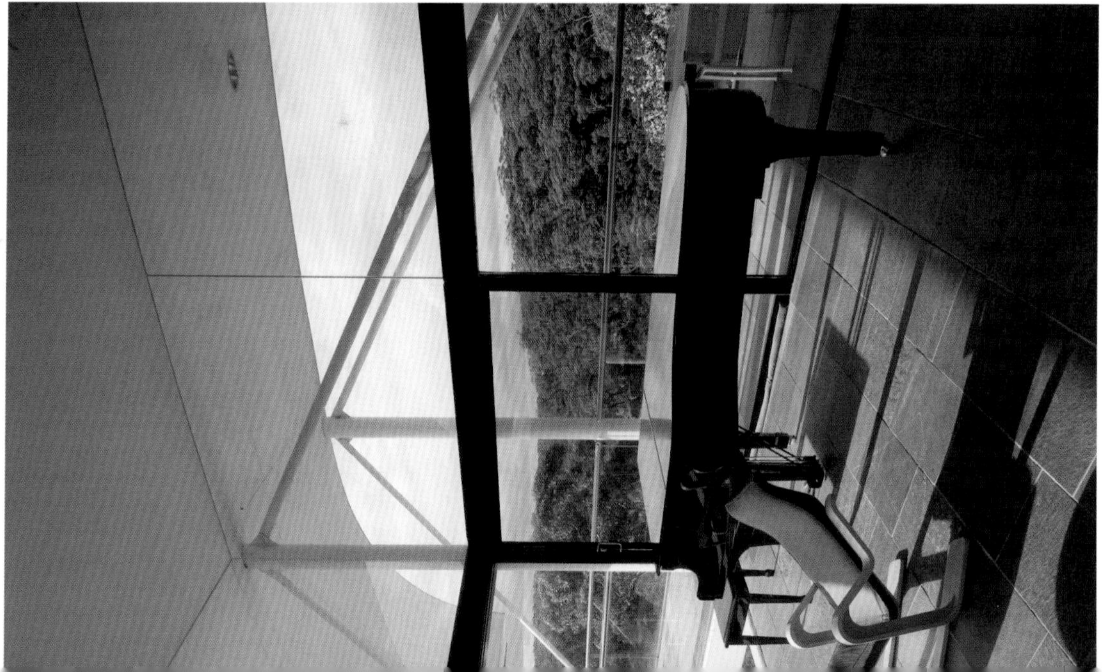

Pretty Beach House
Toby Anderson has turned a once run-down B&B into a national-park-meets-the-sea retreat. Guests have every indulgence catered for, including an outstanding menu by Italian chef Stefano Manfredi for whenever hunger strikes. The decks with heated plunge pools are ideal for relaxing.
High View Road, Pretty Beach,
www.prettybeachhouse.com

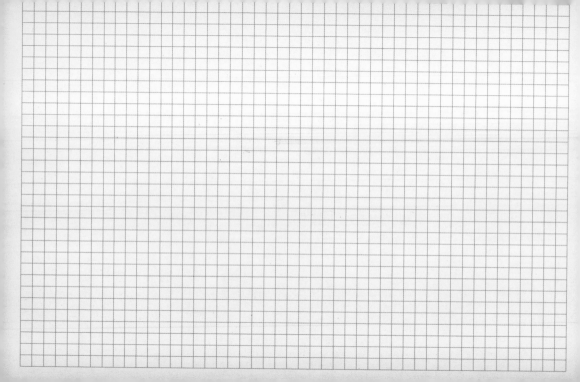

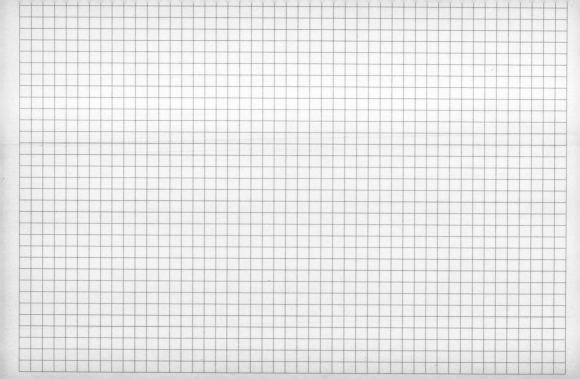

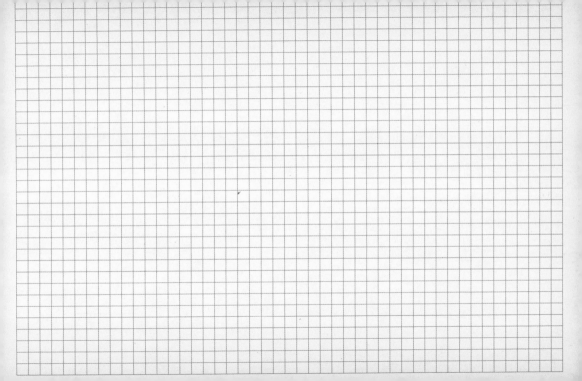

RESOURCES

CITY GUIDE DIRECTORY

A

Aesop 084
Shop 20
The Strand Arcade
412-414 George Street
T 9235 2353
www.aesop.net.au

Akira 072
12a Queen Street
T 9361 5221
www.akira.com.au

Andrew 'Boy' Charlton Pool 088
1C Mrs. Macquaries Road
The Domain
T 9358 6686
www.abcpool.org

Ariel Books 072
42 Oxford Street
T 9332 4581
www.artgallery.nsw.gov.au

Art Gallery of New South Wales 036
Art Gallery Road
T 9225 1744
www.artgallery.nsw.gov.au

Assin 083
T2
Verona Street
T 9331 6265
www.assin.com.au

Aurora Place 012
88 Phillip Street
T 8243 4400
www.auroraplace.com.au

B

Bécasse 053
204 Clarence St
T 9283 3440
www.becasse.com.au

Becker Minty 086
Shop 7
Ikon Building
81 Macleay Street
T 8356 9999
www.beckerminty.com

Becker Minty Woman 086
Cnr Macleay Street and
Greenknowe Avenue
T 8356 9908
www.beckerminty.com

Bentley Restaurant & Bar 047
320 Crown Street
T 9332 2344
www.thebentley.com.au

Bodega Tapas 046
216 Commonwealth Street
T 9212 7766
www.bodegatapas.com

Bondi Icebergs 088
1 Notts Ave
T 9130 3120
www.icebergs.com.au

Bondi Junction 072
500 Oxford Street
T 9619 1111

**Bondi Surf Bathers'
Life Saving Club** 013
Queen Elizabeth Drive
T 9300 9279
www.bondisurfclub.com

Bourke Street Bakery 062
633 Bourke Street
T 9699 1011

BridgeClimb 014
Sydney Harbour Bridge
T 8274 7777
www.bridgeclimb.com

Otto Ristorante Italiano 027
Area 8
6 Cowper Wharf Road
T 9368 7488
www.ottoristorante.com.au

P

Paddington Bazaar 072
St John's Church
Oxford Street
T 9331 2646

Paper Couture 080
284 South Dowling Street
T 9357 6855

Pasteur 062
790 George Street
T 9212 5622

Piano Room 039
Cnr Darlinghurst and Kings Cross Roads
T 9356 8238
www.pianoroom.com.au

Planet 073
114 Commonwealth Street
T 9211 5959
www.planetfurniture.com.au

Pocket Bar 040
13 Burton Street
T 9380 7002

Pretty Beach House 040
High View Road
Pretty Beach
T 4360 1933
www.prettybeachhouse.com

Published Art 076
Shop 2
23½–33 Mary Street
T 9280 2893
www.publishedart.com.au

R

Rambutan 041
96 Oxford Street
T 9360 7772
www.rambutan.com.au

Rockpool Bar & Grill 062
66 Hunter Street
T 8078 1900
www.rockpool.com.au

Rose Seidler House 066
71 Clissold Road
Wahroonga
T 9989 8020
www.hht.net.au/museums

Royal Botanic Gardens 034
Mrs Macquaries Road
T 9231 8111
www.rbgsyd.nsw.gov.au

Ruby Rabbit 058
231 Oxford Street
T 9326 0044
www.rubyrabbit.com.au

The Rum Diaries 052
288 Bondi Rd
T 9300 0440
www.therumdiaries.com.au

S

Saint Augustine Academy 087
642 Bourke Street
T 9690 2863
www.saintaugustineacademy.com.au

Seidler House 100
T 9331 2881
www.contemporaryhotels.com.au

The Shop 033
78 Curlewis Street
T 9365 2600

HOTELS
ADDRESSES AND ROOM RATES

Blue 026
Room rates:
double, A$750;
Wharf Room, A$750;
Suite, from A$1,000
6 Cowper Wharf Road
T 9331 9000
www.tajhotels.com/sydney

Diamant 022
Room rates:
double, from A$150;
Courtyard Room, from A$240;
Courtyard Suite, from A$290;
Penthouse, from A$1,600
14 Kings Cross Road
T 9295 8888
www.diamant.com.au

Establishment 017
Room rates:
double, A$350;
Studio Penthouse Suite, A$970;
Loft Penthouse, A$1,050
5 Bridge Lane
T 9240 3100
www.merivale.com/establishment/hotel

Four Seasons Hotel 016
Room rates:
double, from A$270;
Suite, from A$550
199 George Street
T 9250 3100
www.fourseasons.com/sydney

Fraser Suites 029
Room rates:
Studio Deluxe Suite, from A$217;
One Bedroom Deluxe Suite, from A$246;
Two Bedroom Deluxe Suite, from A$464
488 Kent Street
T 8823 8888
www.sydney.frasershospitality.com

Huski 097
Room rates:
One Bedroom Apartment, from A$380
Sitzmark Street
Falls Creek
Victoria
T 1300 652 260
www.huski.com.au

InterContinental 016
Room rates:
double, A$259;
Penthouse Suite, A$8,000
117 Macquarie Street
T 9253 9000
www.intercontinental.com

Kirketon 020
Room rates:
double, from A$119;
Premium Room, from A$139;
Executive Room, from A$169
229 Darlinghurst Road
T 9332 2011
www.kirketon.com.au

Pretty Beach House 102
Room rates:
price on request
High View Road
Pretty Beach
T 4360 1933
www.prettybeachhouse.com

Ravesi's 028
Room rates:
double, from A$125;
Suite, A$450
Executive Split Level Suite, A$540
Campbell Parade/Hall Street
T 9365 4422
www.ravesis.com.au

Seidler House 100
Room rates:
House, from A$1,200
T 9331 2881
www.contemporaryhotels.com.au

Wolgan Valley 098
Room rates:
suites, from A$1,400
2600 Wolgan Road
Wolgan Valley
www.emirateshotelsresorts.com

WALLPAPER* CITY GUIDES

Editorial Director
Richard Cook

Art Director
Loran Stosskopf

Editors
Rachael Moloney
O'ar Pali

Authors
Carrie Hutchinson

Managing Editor
Jessica Diamond

Senior Designer
Eriko Shimazaki

Designers
Dominic Bell
Ben Blossom
Sara Martin
Ingvild Sandal

Map Illustrator
Russell Bell

Photography Editor
Emma Blau

Photography Assistant
Jasmine Labeau

Sub-Editor
Paul Sentobe

Intern
Hazel Lubbock

Wallpaper* Group

Editor-in-Chief
Tony Chambers

Publishing Director
Gord Ray

Contributors
Paul Barnes
David McKendrick
Meirion Pritchard

Wallpaper* ® is a
registered trademark
of IPC Media Limited

First published 2006
Second edition (revised
and updated) 2010
© 2006 and 2010
IPC Media Limited

ISBN 978 0 7148 5654 4

PHAIDON

Phaidon Press Limited
Regent's Wharf
All Saints Street
London N1 9PA

Phaidon Press Inc
180 Varick Street
New York, NY 10014

Phaidon® is a registered
trademark of Phaidon
Press Limited

www.phaidon.com

A CIP Catalogue record for
this book is available from
the British Library.

All rights reserved.
No part of this publication
may be reproduced, stored
in a retrieval system or
transmitted, in any form
or by any means,
electronic, mechanical,
photocopying, recording
or otherwise, without
the prior permission of
Phaidon Press.

All prices are correct at
time of going to press,
but are subject to change.

Printed in China

PHOTOGRAPHERS

SYDNEY
A COLOUR-CODED GUIDE TO THE CITY'S HOT 'HOODS

BONDI
Babes, beach and great bars. It's not the best surf in Sydney, but it's still unmissable

SURRY HILLS AND DARLINGHURST
Probably the best place for a temporary base, bang in the heart of boho land

WATERLOO
Suburban, although the shops being squeezed out of Surry Hills are opening here

KINGS CROSS AND POTTS POINTS
The sex and sleaze is more sanitised in KC these days. Potts Point is far more genteel

PADDINGTON
Long since gentrified and now the scene of some truly spectacular shopping

THE ROCKS AND CENTRAL BUSINESS DISTRICT
Unusually, Sydney's business district is full of beautiful parks, galleries and eateries

For a full description of each neighbourhood, see the Introduction.
Featured venues are colour-coded, according to the district in which they are located.